START WITH CHINA

How Apple uses cheap labor to
make billions.

SMITH MURPHY & JONES O'KELLY

Preface

"Global Threads: Unraveling the Fabric of Technological Manufacturing"

In the intricate dance of global commerce, where innovation, design, and assembly converge to birth the technological marvels we integrate seamlessly into our lives, lies a narrative often overlooked—the story of how these products come to fruition. "Global Threads" endeavors to unravel the intricacies of technological manufacturing, delving into the multifaceted dimensions that shape the devices we hold in our hands, the laptops perched on our desks, and the gadgets that have become indispensable extensions of our daily existence.

The heartbeat of this exploration lies in the emblematic "Designed in California, Assembled in China" model, a phrase that has transcended its status as a mere statement of origin to become a symbol of the interconnectedness inherent in the technology industry. From the sleek iPhones to the powerful laptops bearing the imprints of Silicon Valley's ingenuity, this model signifies a harmonious collaboration between the technological prowess of innovation hubs like California and the meticulous assembly processes unfolding in manufacturing centers such as China. As we embark on this journey through "Global Threads," our compass is set to navigate the global landscape of technological manufacturing, threading through the tapestry of innovation, consumer perceptions, marketing strategies, and ethical considerations.

Understanding the Globalized Nature of Technological Manufacturing

The "Designed in California, Assembled in China" model serves as our entry point into the labyrinthine world of technological manufacturing. This model, observed across an array of products ranging from smartphones to laptops, reflects a strategic division of labor. California, as a hub of innovation, design, and ideation, shoulders the responsibility of breathing life into groundbreaking concepts. In contrast, China takes center stage in the meticulous assembly processes, where components are intricately woven together to give birth to the final product. The essence of this division is not just geographic; it is a calculated orchestration that optimizes efficiency, leverages specialized expertise, and embodies the collaborative spirit inherent in the global technological supply chain.

Consumer Perceptions

The perceptions held by consumers regarding the "Designed in California, Assembled in China" model are a dynamic tapestry woven by threads of transparency, marketing strategies, and brand image. Our exploration navigates the shifting sands of consumer attitudes, recognizing that these perceptions are not static but evolve with each interaction, each marketing campaign, and each revelation about the practices of companies adopting this model. We delve into the factors influencing consumer choices, acknowledging the intricate dance between perceived product quality, brand reputation, pricing considerations, and the ethical dimensions that have become increasingly significant in shaping modern consumer decisions.

As we examine the impact of marketing strategies, we unravel the artistry of communication. How do companies delicately balance showcasing the innovative spirit of California with the efficiency of Chinese assembly? How does transparent communication influence consumer trust, and what role does the overall brand image play in reinforcing positive perceptions? Through the lens of the consumer, we witness the interplay of factors that transform a mere product into a symbol of innovation, reliability, and ethical consciousness.

Ethical Considerations in the Global Technological Tapestry

In an era where ethical considerations have become integral to consumer decision-making, "Global Threads" examines the ethical implications woven into the very fabric of the "Designed in California, Assembled in China" model. The narrative expands beyond the immediate attributes of the product to scrutinize the conditions in assembly plants, the environmental footprint of the manufacturing process, and the overall social responsibility demonstrated by companies. We explore how consumers, armed with a heightened awareness of global issues, scrutinize the ethical implications of their choices, forcing companies to navigate the delicate terrain where innovation meets responsibility.

Navigating the Global Technological Landscape

Our journey through "Global Threads" is not a mere exploration of manufacturing processes; it is a navigation through the interconnected landscapes of innovation, commerce, and global dynamics. We unravel the complexities of the globalized supply chain, where raw materials traverse continents, components are manufactured in specialized regions, and the final product emerges as a testament to the collaborative efforts of diverse entities. As we navigate this landscape, we encounter the challenges and triumphs of companies seeking to balance innovation with ethical responsibility, seamlessly blending global perspectives into the technological tapestry.

The Intersection of Innovation, Brand Integrity, and Ethical Consciousness

The "Designed in California, Assembled in China" model encapsulates more than a manufacturing strategy; it is a fusion of innovation, brand integrity, and ethical consciousness. "Global Threads" explores how companies, in embracing the globalized nature of manufacturing, are not only delivering cutting-edge products but also crafting narratives that align with the values of modern consumers. We witness the synthesis of these elements defining success in an era where the lines between innovation, brand integrity, and ethical consciousness blur.

Embarking on the Journey

As we embark on this intellectual voyage through "Global Threads," we invite readers to join us in unraveling the intricacies of technological manufacturing. The journey unfolds in chapters that delve into the perceptions of consumers, the strategies employed by companies, and the ethical considerations that echo through the corridors of global commerce. Our compass is set to traverse the intersections of innovation, brand integrity, and ethical consciousness, inviting contemplation on the threads that bind us to the devices we use and the global landscape in which they are conceived.

"Global Threads" is not just a chronicle of manufacturing processes; it is an exploration of the narratives that shape our understanding of technology. We invite readers to engage in this discourse, to question, reflect, and ultimately weave their own threads into the ever-evolving tapestry of technological innovation and its global implications. As we navigate the pages of "Global Threads," may we gain not only a deeper understanding of the intricacies of technological manufacturing but also a heightened awareness of the interconnected world we inhabit—one where innovation, ethics, and commerce intersect, weaving the fabric of our technological future.

Contents

Introduction

In the ever-evolving landscape of technological prowess, Apple Inc. emerges not merely as a beacon of innovation but as an embodiment of strategic mastery and influence. Welcome to "Start with China," an exploration that unravels the intricate tapestry of Apple's triumphs, weaving together global dynamics, economic strategy, and the strategic utilization of labor resources.

The Apple Phenomenon stands as a testament to the seamless integration of ambition, innovation, and strategic finesse. In this narrative journey, Apple's evolution from its humble beginnings to a trillion-dollar giant unfolds as a captivating story. Much like the principles elucidated by Robert Cialdini, Apple goes beyond crafting products—it crafts desires. The company leverages design excellence to forge an emotional connection that transcends the transactional nature of its offerings.

Globalization and Outsourcing form a symphony of influence in Apple's trajectory. As the company extends its manufacturing embrace to China, we delve into the intricate psychology behind this global dance, exploring the principles of influence that guide such strategic decisions. It transcends mere economics; it is the art of crafting a narrative that shapes perception and influences markets.

In this captivating realm of Apple's triumphs, success isn't confined to sales figures and market share. It is a carefully orchestrated dance of desire and innovation. As Cialdini delves into the psychology of influence, Apple too engages in the art of crafting desire. Products cease to be mere commodities; they transform into coveted symbols, and the Apple logo becomes a beacon of aspiration.

Join us as we explore the design excellence that transcends functionality, creating a sensory experience beyond the tangible. We unravel the allure of Apple's innovations, from the groundbreaking Macintosh to the game-changing iPhone, each a testament to the company's disruptive prowess in shaping the technological landscape.

At the crossroads of Apple's success lies a strategic decision to globalize and outsource, particularly to China. It's not just about reducing production costs; it's a nuanced dance of influence and economic strategy. Cialdini's principles come to life as we uncover the psychology behind this strategic move, where the utilization of cheap labor becomes a pivotal note in the symphony of global dynamics.

Embark with us on a journey through economic considerations, intricate supply chain dynamics, and the profound implications of cheap labor on efficiency. The role of cheap labor ceases to be merely logistical; it becomes a strategic element in the narrative Apple weaves about itself and its products.

As we traverse the landscapes of innovation and labor dynamics, consider the interconnected nature of Apple's success. Through the lens of Cialdini's principles, we decipher the psychological tactics employed in creating not just products but a brand that influences perceptions and shapes consumer behavior. Step into the world where desire meets strategy, and innovation seamlessly blends with the global dance of economics.

Join us on this intellectual journey, where the lines between strategy, psychology, and corporate prowess blur, revealing the interplay of influence, innovation, and the role of cheap labor in turning visionary ideas into global empires.

Chapter 1: The Genesis of Apple's Strategy

In the vast tapestry of corporate strategy, the story of Apple's genesis unfolds as a multifaceted narrative, blending visionary leadership, innovative thinking, and strategic foresight. This extensive chapter delves deeply into the foundational elements that set the stage for Apple's trajectory, offering a comprehensive exploration of its birth, the formative years, and the profound influence of its co-founder, Steve Jobs.

The Birth of Apple | The inception of Apple Inc. is a riveting tale that unfolds within the unassuming confines of a garage—a space that would later become synonymous with innovation and technological breakthroughs. Born from the collaborative minds of Steve Jobs, Steve Wozniak, and Ronald Wayne, Apple emerged as a disruptive force in the burgeoning tech landscape. This section takes a meticulous journey through the early days of Apple, providing a nuanced understanding of the challenges, experiments, and the nascent vision that fueled the company's inception.

The Early Years and Vision | As Apple took its inaugural steps, it became a beacon of visionary thinking, challenging the conventional boundaries of computing. Jobs and Wozniak envisioned a future where the power of computing would be democratized, placing it directly into the hands of individuals. This subsection offers an in-depth exploration of the early projects that shaped Apple's identity, the hurdles faced, and the crystallization of a vision that would redefine the role of technology in our lives.

Steve Jobs' Influence | Central to Apple's early narrative is the charismatic and visionary Steve Jobs, whose influence permeated every facet of the company's strategy. This segment delves into the profound impact of Jobs on Apple's corporate culture, its philosophy of product design, and the relentless pursuit of excellence that became ingrained in the brand's DNA. By examining Jobs' role as a driving force, we uncover the nuances of his leadership style and the lasting legacy he left on Apple's strategic landscape.

Globalization and Outsourcing | In the evolution of Apple's strategy, globalization and outsourcing emerge as transformative and far-reaching elements that shape the company's trajectory. This section expands extensively on the strategic decision to shift manufacturing operations to China, unraveling the complexities, motivations, and implications of this pivotal move.

Shifting Manufacturing to China | Apple's strategic pivot to shift manufacturing operations to China represents a watershed moment in the company's history. This subsection provides an intricate exploration of the factors that propelled Apple to embrace this international strategy, the advantages it sought, and the nuanced considerations that underscored this significant decision. The move to China marked a strategic recalibration that reverberated through the industry, setting the stage for Apple's global prominence.

"According to Apple, 1.5 million people work in their supply chain, a third of which work in "final assembly" mega-factories. This means that during the same three months Apple set these financial

records, 1 million Apple workers made the parts for these phones and 500,000 put them together.

Workers at one assembly factory make base wages of 1530 yuan ($244) per month (This is the minimum wage in Suzhou, China). With lots overtime, workers can increase these earnings to roughly 3650 yuan ($582) per month, according to a 2014 investigation by Students and Scholars Against Corporate Misbehaviour (SACOM). This was at Pegatron, one of Apple's main suppliers in China, which handles the final assembly of Apple's iPhones. Other final assembly plants include Foxconn and Quanta. The living wage in China, as calculated by the Asia Floor Wage in 2013, is approximately 4537 yuan ($725 USD, PPP). This is based on working 48 hours per week at a rate of about $3.77 per hour.

However, workers in Apple's supplier factories, do not work 48 hours per week, especially during peak production times. SACOM's investigation found that some workers at Pegatron worked for 10 weeks without a rest day and often for 12-15 hours a day, sometimes up to 17-18 hours a day. This means that during peak production time, workers at Pegatron were working between 84 and 105 hours per week. This is more than double a typical workweek around the world.

Taking a conservative estimate of (12 hours/day, 30 days per month) workers earn approximately 10.13 yuan/hour, or roughly $1.62 per hour. This is less than half the recommended living wage of about 3.77 per hour. According to a 2008 study published by MIT's Sloan school of Business, which looked at the value chain of iPods, the assembly time required for one device was 10 minutes, or six iPods per hour. Which means, if comparable, the cost of labor per iPhone assembled is roughly 27 cents.

Apple's profit margin, or the money in pure profit it makes on every iPhone sold, is 39.9%, according to BBC. The industry average for *consumer electronics is below 10%, according to Standard & Poor's. The iPhone 6 costs between $199 and $749 at Apple's online store, which means that depending on which phone you buy and the amount of storage you elect, Apple could be pocketing somewhere between $79 and $299 in profit. Apple's margins are high for any sector, let alone a sector that requires the work of millions of human beings to make a product. The per piece labor of just $0.27 (for assembly) helps explain how Apple is able to achieve these remarkable margins.*

Labor is one of the highest costs that any business will incur in any sector. One of the reasons, and usually the primary reason, a business may choose to manufacture in one particular country is the relative "cheapness" of labor costs there—meaning low wages. But at what point does the pursuit of lower wages move from a "savvy business scheme" to full-on exploitation? In China, where Apple's iPhones are made, wages are relatively low. So low in fact that workers must rely on overtime pay to get by. Electronics brands argue that workers like to work overtime so they can save for their future, but if workers base wages were raised to provide a living wage to begin with, would they elect to work such exhausting hours?

In these mega-electronics factories, there are typically 2 shifts, day and night. Workers either work 12 hours during the day, or 12 hours straight through the night. This often does not include time that workers may need to dress/undress, pass through security, or attend pre- or post-shift meetings. With either shift, little time is left over for recreation, personal development, or even rest." - www.greenamerica.org

Impact on Costs and Efficiency | As manufacturing transcended geographical borders, the repercussions on Apple's financial landscape became increasingly pronounced. This part scrutinizes the economic considerations that underpinned the decision to globalize manufacturing, offering a detailed analysis of the cost efficiencies gained and the subsequent enhancement of overall operational efficiency. The globalization of Apple's manufacturing operations marked a paradigm shift in the industry, influencing not only the company's financial standing but also its market positioning and supply chain dynamics.

$74.6 billion revenue

$18 billion in pure profit

$142 billion net cash reserves

74.5 million iPhones sold

Apple fiscal Q1 numbers, as reported by BBC

On this expansive exploration of Apple's strategic genesis—a journey that not only uncovers the roots of the company's success but also offers an intricate analysis of the visionary influence of Steve Jobs and the strategic decisions that laid the foundation for Apple's ascent to global prominence.

Chapter 2: The Power of Cheap Labor: Navigating Labor Economics and Apple's Manufacturing Partnerships

In the labyrinthine landscape of Apple's global strategy, the strategic deployment of cheap labor emerges as a pivotal and intricate element, shaping the dynamics of labor economics and influencing the character of the company's manufacturing partnerships. This expansive chapter undertakes a comprehensive exploration of the complexities surrounding cheap labor, delving into its far-reaching impact on both global and localized scales. Additionally, we scrutinize Apple's key manufacturing partnerships in China, illuminating the intricacies of labor practices and conditions that define the company's engagement with cheap labor.

Labor Economics: Understanding the Nuances of Cheap Labor

Labor economics is a multifaceted field that extends beyond the conventional metrics of cost and efficiency. In this section, we embark on an in-depth exploration of the intricate dynamics that underpin the concept of cheap labor, transcending its superficial association with reduced costs.

Understanding Cheap Labor | Cheap labor, often reduced to a financial metric, embodies a complex interplay of socio-economic factors, market conditions, and global competition. We dissect the nuanced layers of this term, delving into economic theories and practical realities that define the concept. By examining how cheap labor interacts with broader economic trends, we seek to foster a profound understanding of the intricate relationships between labor, production costs, and global market dynamics.

Pros and Cons | The utilization of cheap labor, like any economic strategy, presents both advantages and challenges. In this subsection, we meticulously examine the multifaceted nature of the pros and cons associated with tapping into inexpensive labor pools. From cost savings and increased production capacity to potential ethical concerns and socio-economic impacts, we navigate through the dichotomy of cheap labor, offering a balanced perspective on its implications for corporations and the broader workforce.

The Foxconn Saga: Balancing Cost Efficiency and Ethical Concerns

As a prime example of the impact of cheap labor, the case study explores Apple's longstanding partnership with Foxconn, a major manufacturing partner in China. Delving into the historical context, we scrutinize how cost efficiencies were achieved while addressing the ethical concerns surrounding labor practices. The Foxconn case study serves as a lens through which we examine the delicate equilibrium between the advantages of cheap labor and the imperative to uphold ethical standards.

"In a widely cited anecdote about the power of the Chinese workforce, a manager at an iPhone factory was once able to rally 8,000 workers from their dormitories to do a 12-hour shift at short notice, with nothing more than an offer of a cup of tea and some biscuits. Apple urgently required a refit on a new iPhone model, and within a week production was back on track.

The unrivalled discipline, efficiency and reliability of Chinese workers, as illustrated by the anecdote, convinced Apple – the largest US consumer electronics company – to outsource its iPhone assembly to China – and stick with that decision despite rising labour costs, human rights controversies and more recently intensified rivalry between Beijing and Washington.

Foxconn Technology Group's factory in Zhengzhou, capital of central Henan province, was designed to take advantage of China's highly organised labour force. The vast compound – known as "iPhone City" – can accommodate up to 300,000 workers who live in on-site dormitories in nearby residential high-rise buildings. This army of young workers – men and women in their 20s and 30s – have made China an integral part of Apple's supply chain." - Ben Jiang, Iris Deng, et al. (Inside Foxconn's 'iPhone City': how Apple's biggest contractor fell victim to China's zero-Covid policy)

Apple's Manufacturing Partnerships in China: A Strategic Nexus of Global Production

Central to Apple's global supply chain is the strategic deployment of manufacturing partnerships, particularly in China. In this section, we unravel the intricate web of collaborations that defines Apple's manufacturing ecosystem, focusing on the company's key partnerships and their pivotal role in shaping production capabilities.

Overview of Key Partnerships | A nuanced understanding of Apple's manufacturing alliances in China is essential to decoding the intricacies of the company's production dynamics. This subsection navigates through the key partnerships that have played a transformative role in shaping Apple's manufacturing landscape. From Pegatron to Quanta Computer, we explore the synergies, challenges, and strategic alignments that have evolved over time.

Labor Practices and Conditions | Moving beyond quantitative metrics, this part scrutinizes the qualitative aspects of Apple's manufacturing partnerships, with a specific focus on labor practices and conditions. Through an in-depth exploration, we aim to uncover the working conditions, ethical considerations, and the broader socio-economic impact of Apple's engagement with cheap labor in China. labor practices and conditions stand as the cornerstone of ethical and responsible corporate conduct. This essay delves into the multifaceted realm of how companies, particularly exemplified by Apple, navigate the complexities of labor, scrutinizing practices and conditions in manufacturing hubs like China. The exploration aims to unravel the human dimension of global production, shedding light on the challenges, advancements, and ethical considerations that define the labor landscape.

Global companies, especially those with extensive supply chains like Apple, operate within a complex framework of labor practices that govern the relationship between employers and employees. The understanding of labor practices necessitates a comprehensive view that encompasses policies, procedures, and standards. For Apple, this involves navigating diverse labor laws, cultural nuances, and ethical benchmarks as it operates on a global scale. The harmonization of practices across diverse jurisdictions becomes a crucial aspect of Apple's strategy in dealing with the intricacies of global labor practices.

Compliance with local regulations is a central theme in Apple's approach to labor practices. Balancing global corporate standards with the unique labor frameworks of each manufacturing hub is a delicate task. The company must navigate a complex web of regional labor regulations, ensuring that its operations align with the diverse legal requirements of different countries. The ability to adhere to local regulations while maintaining a cohesive global approach is indicative of Apple's commitment to ethical and responsible labor practices.

In the contemporary manufacturing landscape, the demand for transparency and accountability in labor practices has witnessed a significant upswing. Stakeholders, including consumers, advocacy groups, and regulatory bodies, increasingly scrutinize companies for their commitment to ethical manufacturing. Apple, recognizing the importance of transparency, has undertaken initiatives to enhance accountability in its supply chain. This includes regular supplier audits, transparent disclosure practices, and partnerships with third-party organizations to ensure adherence to ethical labor standards.

Improving working conditions has become a focal point for companies aiming to foster a positive and sustainable work environment. Apple, in its commitment to the well-being of its workforce, extends its focus beyond mere compliance. The emphasis is on creating a workplace that not only meets regulatory standards but goes beyond to ensure the safety, health, and overall well-being of its employees. This holistic approach reflects a dedication to fostering a positive and sustainable work environment, aligning with evolving societal expectations regarding labor practices.

In conclusion, labor practices and conditions form an integral aspect of global manufacturing, particularly for companies with expansive supply chains like Apple. Navigating the complexities of diverse labor frameworks, balancing global standards with local regulations, and embracing transparency and accountability are central tenets of Apple's approach. The commitment to improving working conditions goes beyond compliance, reflecting a dedication to the holistic well-being of the workforce. As the global manufacturing landscape continues to evolve, the ethical and responsible treatment of labor remains a cornerstone for companies seeking to thrive in an interconnected and socially conscious world.

Case Study 2: Luxshare Precision - A Tale of Innovation and Labor Dynamics

As a second case study, we delve into the strategic partnership between Apple and Luxshare Precision, a rising star in the manufacturing landscape. This case study explores how Luxshare's innovative approach to labor management has influenced Apple's production capabilities. By examining Luxshare's practices and conditions, we gain insights into a dynamic collaboration that mirrors the evolving landscape of global labor dynamics.

"The manufacturer is also making production preparations for Apple Vision Pro, a wearable headset device that will be available early next year, chairwoman Wang Laichun told state-backed newspaper The Paper. Luxshare has increased the production types and numbers of Apple's iPhone products in recent years, Wang added.

"Luxshare is continuing to expand its production capacity in China to meet Apple's needs," Wang said, adding the company built a new plant in Kunshan last year to support the development and mass production of iPhone.

Join us on this expansive exploration of the power dynamics inherent in the utilization of cheap labor—a chapter that not only unravels the intricacies of labor economics but also sheds light on the real-world implications of Apple's manufacturing partnerships in China. As we navigate the nuanced terrain of global supply chains and labor dynamics, we invite you to consider the multifaceted nature of the choices corporations make in pursuit of efficiency and cost-effectiveness. Through the lens of case studies, we aim to provide a deeper understanding of the complexities that underpin the strategic utilization of cheap labor in the globalized production landscape.

Chapter 3: The Innovation-Exploitation Dilemma

In the dynamic landscape of global business, the balance between innovation and exploitation poses a complex dilemma for corporations. This chapter delves into the intricacies of the Innovation-Exploitation Dilemma, exploring the tension between fostering innovation and leveraging existing resources.

It will be examined through the lens of the Innovation Paradox, discussing how companies, including Apple, navigate this delicate equilibrium. Additionally, we will explore success stories beyond Apple, examining case studies of companies that effectively leverage cheap labor while addressing ethical considerations.

The Innovation Paradox | The paradox of innovation within the realm of corporate strategy is a dynamic interplay between two fundamental approaches to growth: innovation and exploitation.

This paradox materializes from the inherent tension between these strategies—where innovation propels competitiveness, exploitation strategically capitalizes on existing resources and processes. The crux lies in achieving a delicate equilibrium, as finding the right balance becomes paramount for sustained success in the ever-evolving business landscape.

In the context of corporate growth, innovation and exploitation emerge as distinct but complementary strategies. Innovation entails the introduction of novel ideas, products, or processes that have the potential to disrupt markets and establish a competitive advantage.

On the contrary, exploitation involves the maximization of efficiency and profitability derived from existing resources and established practices. Both strategies are integral to a company's growth trajectory, but the challenge lies in effectively managing and reconciling the dichotomy between them.

Innovation serves as a catalyst for corporate competitiveness, driving organizations to push boundaries, explore new territories, and constantly evolve. The pursuit of innovation is characterized by a forward-looking mindset, a commitment to R&D, and a willingness to take calculated risks. Successful innovation positions a company as a market leader, enabling it to differentiate itself from competitors and meet evolving customer demands.

On the other hand, exploitation involves optimizing the utility of existing resources, processes, and market positions. It is a strategy centered around refining and maximizing the efficiency of current operations. This could encompass streamlining production processes, optimizing supply chain logistics, or leveraging existing brand equity to capture a larger market share. Exploitation is grounded in the maximization of immediate gains and the extraction of value from established assets.

The tension between innovation and exploitation gives rise to the Innovation Paradox, a phenomenon that demands strategic finesse from corporations. This paradox is not a binary choice between the two strategies but a dynamic interplay where companies must effectively balance their innovation and exploitation portfolios. Striking the right equilibrium is not a one-size-fits-all endeavor; instead, it is a nuanced process that varies based on industry dynamics, market conditions, and the organization's own strengths and weaknesses.

The Innovation Paradox underscores the challenge of managing both short-term gains and long-term sustainability. Overemphasis on innovation might result in neglecting established revenue streams, leading to financial instability. Conversely, an excessive focus on exploitation can lead to complacency, making the organization vulnerable to disruptive innovations from competitors. The delicate dance between these two strategies is a continual process of adaptation and strategic decision-making.

For companies aiming for sustained success, the Innovation Paradox necessitates a strategic approach that embraces both innovation and exploitation. Achieving this balance involves recognizing that these strategies are not mutually exclusive but complementary components of a holistic growth strategy. A company's ability to leverage innovation to drive competitiveness while simultaneously optimizing existing resources defines its resilience and adaptability in a rapidly changing business landscape.

Examining the success stories of companies beyond Apple provides valuable insights into how organizations navigate the complexities of the Innovation-Exploitation Dilemma. Nike, for instance, stands out as a case study of a company that has effectively leveraged cheap labor while also addressing ethical considerations. The company strategically expanded its global manufacturing footprint to benefit from cost advantages while implementing initiatives to ensure fair labor practices and environmental responsibility.

Ethical considerations play a pivotal role in the Innovation-Exploitation Dilemma, particularly when it comes to leveraging cheap labor. Companies that successfully navigate this dilemma prioritize responsible business practices and transparently address concerns related to worker conditions, fair wages, and environmental impact. The pursuit of corporate success is not divorced from ethical imperatives, and organizations that uphold high ethical standards are better positioned to thrive in the long run.

Innovation encapsulated in the Innovation-Exploitation Dilemma is a dynamic challenge that defines the strategic landscape for corporations. Balancing the pursuit of innovation with the optimization of existing resources requires a nuanced approach that recognizes the complementary nature of these strategies. The Innovation Paradox calls for a strategic dance, where companies navigate the tension between immediate gains and long-term sustainability.

Examining success stories and ethical considerations beyond Apple enriches our understanding of how organizations effectively manage this delicate equilibrium, showcasing that the path to sustained success is paved with strategic adaptation, ethical leadership, and a commitment to innovation and exploitation as complementary facets of a holistic growth strategy.

Innovations vs. Exploitation | The duality between innovation and exploitation represents a pivotal dynamic within the corporate landscape, each embodying distinct strategies for organizational growth. The intricate interplay between these two approaches lies at the heart of corporate evolution, where innovation encompasses the introduction of new ideas, products, or processes, disrupting the market and creating a competitive edge. In contrast, exploitation centers on maximizing the efficiency and profitability of existing resources and established practices. Both innovation and exploitation are indispensable for a company's survival, and the complexity emerges in the strategic allocation of resources between these two realms.

Innovation serves as a catalyst for organizational progress, representing the pursuit of novel ideas that have the potential to redefine industries and market landscapes. This multifaceted concept extends beyond the mere introduction of new products; it encapsulates a mindset of continuous improvement, adaptability, and a commitment to pushing the boundaries of what is possible. The innovative endeavors of a company are characterized by forward-thinking initiatives, investments in research and development (R&D), and a willingness to embark on calculated risks.

One of the primary objectives of innovation is to disrupt the market, introducing elements that challenge the status quo and propel the organization ahead of its competitors. This disruption is not confined to product innovation alone; it extends to novel business models, groundbreaking processes, and transformative approaches to customer engagement. Innovation is the driving force behind companies that aspire not only to meet but to anticipate and exceed customer expectations.

Exploitation, on the other hand, is rooted in the optimization of existing resources and well-established practices. It is a strategic approach that revolves around refining and maximizing the efficiency of current operations. This can encompass streamlining production processes, optimizing supply chain logistics, or leveraging the brand equity of existing products to capture a larger market share. Exploitation is grounded in the maximization of immediate gains and the extraction of value from established assets.

The paradox between innovation and exploitation lies in the strategic orchestration of these two seemingly divergent approaches. Both are essential for a company's growth and sustainability, but the challenge arises in determining how to allocate resources effectively between them. This challenge is not a dichotomy but a dynamic interplay, a continuum where organizations must strike a balance that aligns with their unique goals, industry dynamics, and the broader economic landscape.

To delve deeper into the essence of innovation, it is essential to recognize that innovation is not confined to a singular dimension. While product innovation is a prominent aspect, innovation permeates various facets of organizational functioning. Process innovation involves optimizing internal workflows, enhancing operational efficiency, and embracing technologies that streamline organizational processes. Business model innovation entails reimagining how a company creates, delivers, and captures value, often leading to transformative shifts in market positioning.

Moreover, innovation is inherently linked to adaptability and resilience. In a rapidly evolving business environment, companies that embrace innovation are better equipped to navigate uncertainties and capitalize on emerging opportunities. The pursuit of innovation is not a one-time event but an ongoing process that requires organizational agility, a culture of experimentation, and a readiness to learn from both successes and failures.

Contrastingly, exploitation represents a strategic focus on deriving maximum value from existing resources and practices. This approach is anchored in optimizing the efficiency of current operations to achieve short-term gains. Exploitation involves a meticulous examination of internal processes, supply chain logistics, and market positioning to identify areas where incremental improvements can be made. By leveraging established assets, companies can capitalize on their existing market presence and enhance their competitive advantage.

The Innovation-Exploitation Dilemma underscores the need for companies to navigate the tension between immediate gains and long-term sustainability. Overemphasis on innovation, while neglecting established revenue streams, can lead to financial instability. Conversely, an excessive focus on exploitation may result in complacency, making the organization vulnerable to disruptive innovations from competitors. Achieving the right equilibrium requires strategic acumen, adaptability, and a keen understanding of the organization's unique strengths and weaknesses.

To illuminate the dynamics of the Innovation-Exploitation Dilemma, it is instructive to explore real-world examples that showcase the successful orchestration of these strategies. Apple, often lauded as a pioneer in innovation, provides a compelling case study. The company's introduction of groundbreaking products such as the iPhone and iPad exemplifies its commitment to innovation, propelling it to the forefront of the technology industry.

Simultaneously, Apple has demonstrated an adeptness in exploitation by leveraging the success of its products to build a robust ecosystem. The company's ability to create an interconnected ecosystem of devices, services, and software represents a strategic exploitation of its existing market presence. By optimizing the efficiency of its supply chain and maximizing the value derived from its product offerings, Apple has achieved sustained success in both innovation and exploitation.

Another illustrative example is Amazon, a company renowned for its innovative approach to e-commerce. Amazon continually disrupts the retail landscape through innovations such as one-click purchasing, drone delivery, and voice-activated shopping. Simultaneously, the company excels in exploitation by optimizing its logistics and supply chain operations to achieve unparalleled efficiency in product delivery. The strategic balance between innovation and exploitation has propelled Amazon to the forefront of the e-commerce industry.

The success stories of companies like Apple and Amazon highlight the nuanced and dynamic nature of the Innovation-Exploitation Dilemma. These companies have navigated the paradox by strategically allocating resources between innovation and exploitation based on their organizational goals, market dynamics, and the evolving needs of their customers. Their ability to seamlessly integrate both approaches has been instrumental in achieving sustained growth and competitiveness.

In navigating the Innovation-Exploitation Dilemma, organizations must recognize that the optimal balance is not a static endpoint but a continual process of adaptation. The strategic emphasis on innovation and exploitation may shift over time, necessitating a flexible and responsive approach. Companies should foster a culture that encourages experimentation, embraces change, and values continuous learning.

Moreover, the Innovation-Exploitation Dilemma is not solely applicable to large corporations; it is equally relevant to startups and small businesses. For emerging enterprises, the challenge lies in managing resource constraints while simultaneously fostering innovation and exploiting existing opportunities. Startups often face the pressure to innovate rapidly to establish a foothold in the market, but they must also strategically exploit their unique strengths to gain a competitive edge.

Ethical considerations play a pivotal role in navigating the Innovation-Exploitation Dilemma, especially when it comes to leveraging cheap labor. Companies that successfully manage this dilemma prioritize responsible business practices and transparently address concerns related to worker conditions, fair wages, and environmental impact. Ethical considerations are integral to sustaining long-term success, as consumers and stakeholders increasingly value companies that uphold high ethical standards.

In conclusion, the Innovation-Exploitation Dilemma encapsulates the strategic challenge of managing the dynamic tension between innovation and exploitation. The paradox lies not in choosing one strategy over the other but in orchestrating a nuanced and adaptive balance between the two. Innovation propels companies forward, disrupts markets, and ensures long-term adaptability.

Balancing Act for Corporations | Corporations must walk a tightrope between fostering innovation and exploiting existing strengths. Overemphasis on either side can lead to challenges. Too much focus on innovation may result in neglecting current revenue streams, while excessive exploitation may lead to stagnation and vulnerability to disruptive competitors. Successful companies navigate this paradox by strategically managing their innovation and exploitation portfolios.

Success Stories Beyond Apple | While Apple is often cited as a benchmark for innovation, numerous companies have successfully navigated the Innovation-Exploitation Dilemma, particularly when leveraging cheap labor. Examining these success stories provides valuable insights into effective strategies and ethical considerations.

Case Studies of Companies Leveraging Cheap Labor:

Several companies have thrived by strategically leveraging cheap labor without compromising ethical standards. One such case study is Nike, which expanded its global manufacturing footprint to benefit from cost advantages while implementing initiatives to address labor rights and environmental concerns. This example showcases how companies can effectively exploit global resources while prioritizing responsible business practices.

Ethical Considerations | The use of cheap labor often raises ethical considerations, including concerns about worker conditions, fair wages, and environmental impact. Companies that successfully navigate the Innovation-Exploitation Dilemma address these concerns transparently and proactively. This section explores the ethical dimensions of leveraging cheap labor, emphasizing the importance of responsible business practices in the pursuit of corporate success.

The Innovation-Exploitation Dilemma is a fundamental challenge faced by corporations seeking sustained growth. Striking the right balance between innovation and exploitation is a delicate but necessary endeavor. Examining success stories beyond Apple provides valuable insights into effective strategies, especially when leveraging cheap labor. Companies that navigate this dilemma successfully do so by embracing a strategic balance, prioritizing ethical considerations, and adapting to the evolving demands of the global business landscape.

Chapter 4: Psychological Tactics in Corporate Strategies

In the intricate landscape of corporate strategies, the utilization of psychological tactics plays a pivotal role in shaping consumer behavior, influencing market dynamics, and establishing brand prominence. This chapter delves into the realm of psychological tactics, focusing on the application of Robert Cialdini's principles. These principles, namely Reciprocity, Commitment, Social Proof, Authority, Liking, and Scarcity, serve as powerful tools in the strategic arsenal of corporations. The exploration will extend to how Apple, as a prominent player in the corporate arena, leverages these psychological principles to craft compelling strategies that resonate with consumers and shape market perceptions.

Applying Robert Cialdini's Principles

Reciprocity

Reciprocity, a fundamental principle in social psychology, centers on the idea of exchanging favors or gifts. In the corporate context, the concept of reciprocity is harnessed to create a sense of obligation. Companies offer value, whether in the form of products, services, or personalized experiences, with the expectation that consumers will reciprocate by engaging positively with the brand.

Commitment

The principle of commitment relies on the human tendency to align actions with established commitments. Corporations strategically leverage this principle by encouraging small initial commitments from consumers. Once individuals make a commitment, they are more likely to follow through with further actions that align with their initial commitment. This psychological tactic forms the foundation for building brand loyalty and long-term engagement.

Social Proof

Social Proof draws on the inherent human inclination to align behavior with the perceived actions of others. In the corporate realm, this principle is manifested through testimonials, user reviews, and endorsements. Companies strategically showcase positive experiences and endorsements from other consumers to create a sense of social validation, influencing prospective customers to follow suit.

Authority

Authority taps into the tendency of individuals to defer to perceived expertise. In corporate strategies, establishing and showcasing authority is a means of influencing consumer trust and confidence. Companies often leverage authoritative figures, expert endorsements, or industry recognition to position themselves as credible and trustworthy sources, thereby shaping consumer perceptions.

Liking

Liking is grounded in the concept that individuals are more likely to engage with and be influenced by those they like. Corporations strategically deploy this principle by humanizing their brand, connecting with consumers on a personal level, and creating a positive emotional association. The likability factor is a powerful tool in building strong brand affinity and fostering enduring customer relationships.

Scarcity

The principle of Scarcity capitalizes on the psychological impact of limited availability. By emphasizing the scarcity or exclusivity of a product or service, corporations instill a sense of urgency in consumers. This tactic encourages prompt decision-making and heightened interest, as individuals are motivated to secure something perceived as rare or exclusive.

How Apple Utilizes these Principles

Reciprocity at Apple

Apple excels in the principle of reciprocity by offering free trials, personalized product recommendations, and exclusive content through its ecosystem. By providing value upfront, Apple cultivates a sense of reciprocity, fostering a loyal customer base that is more likely to engage with its products and services.

Commitment in Apple's Approach

Apple strategically employs commitment by encouraging users to create Apple IDs, customize preferences, and establish an integrated digital presence. Once users commit to these initial steps, they are more likely to continue using Apple products and services, creating a seamless and interconnected experience across devices.

Social Proof in Apple's Marketing

Apple leverages social proof through its marketing strategies, prominently featuring user testimonials, reviews, and endorsements from influential figures. The "Shot on iPhone" campaign, showcasing user-generated content, is a prime example. By highlighting positive experiences, Apple creates a social proof narrative that influences consumer perceptions.

Authority in Apple's Branding

Apple positions itself as an authority in the technology industry through a combination of sleek design, cutting-edge innovation, and strategic partnerships. Endorsements from tech experts, influencers, and industry awards reinforce Apple's authority, instilling confidence in consumers and solidifying its position as a leading brand.

Liking and Humanizing the Apple Brand

Apple excels in the likability factor by humanizing its brand. The "Get a Mac" campaign featuring Justin Long and John Hodgman showcased the relatable, personified characters of Mac and PC. This approach fosters a friendly and approachable image, making Apple products not just technologically superior but also emotionally appealing.

Scarcity in Apple's Product Releases

Apple's product release strategy is a masterclass in utilizing scarcity. The limited availability of new products, combined with the anticipation generated through carefully orchestrated announcements, creates a sense of exclusivity. Consumers eagerly await new releases, and the perceived scarcity enhances the desirability of Apple's offerings.

The application of Robert Cialdini's psychological principles in corporate strategies, exemplified through Apple's practices, underscores the nuanced and deliberate efforts to shape consumer behavior. Reciprocity, commitment, social proof, authority, liking, and scarcity serve as potent tools that, when strategically deployed, contribute to building brand loyalty, influencing purchasing decisions, and establishing a positive market perception. Apple's adept use of these principles exemplifies how a company can not only deliver exceptional products but also craft a compelling narrative that resonates with consumers on a psychological level.

Chapter 5: The Consumer Perspective

In unraveling the intricate tapestry of corporate strategies, it is imperative to shift the lens towards the consumer perspective. This chapter delves into the nuanced intricacies of how consumers perceive the "Designed in California, Assembled in China" model, dissecting the role of marketing strategies, the impact on brand image, and the profound choices consumers make in the realm of ethical considerations. As we traverse through the consumer landscape, we gain insights into the multifaceted dynamics that influence purchasing decisions and the evolving role of ethical considerations in shaping consumer preferences.

Perception of the "Designed in California, Assembled in China" Model

The paradigm of the "Designed in California, Assembled in China" model stands as a symbol of the globalized nature inherent in the technology industry's manufacturing processes. This model, observed across a spectrum of products from smartphones to laptops, delineates a distinct division of labor. Here, the realms of design and innovation unfold within technology hubs like California, while the intricate assembly processes find realization in manufacturing centers such as China. The perceptions held by consumers regarding this model are nuanced and intricate, shaped by a multitude of factors that extend beyond the tangible product itself. This exploration delves into the complexities surrounding the consumer perspective on the "Designed in California, Assembled in China" model, examining the impact of marketing strategies, the cultivation of brand image, and the overarching influence of ethical considerations in the evolving landscape of consumer choices.

The essence of the "Designed in California, Assembled in China" model encapsulates more than just the geographical coordinates of its origin and assembly. It embodies a strategic approach to manufacturing, capitalizing on the strengths of different regions to create a harmonious synergy. The conceptual core lies in the division of tasks, with California contributing to the ideation, innovation, and design phases, and China taking the helm in the meticulous assembly processes. This bifurcation optimizes efficiency, leverages specialized expertise, and contributes to the global interconnectedness of the technology supply chain.

Consumer perceptions of the "Designed in California, Assembled in China" model are not static; rather, they are shaped by a dynamic interplay of factors. One crucial determinant is the clarity and transparency with which companies communicate their manufacturing approach. The degree of information provided to consumers, from the sourcing of materials to the conditions in assembly plants, influences their understanding and, subsequently, their perceptions. Additionally, the brand image cultivated by companies, their reputation for quality, and the overall consumer trust in the brand contribute significantly to how the "Designed in California, Assembled in China" model is perceived.

The strategic deployment of marketing strategies becomes a linchpin in shaping consumer perceptions. Companies adopting this model must navigate the delicate balance of highlighting the technological prowess emanating from California and the efficiency brought about by Chinese assembly. Transparent communication regarding the collaboration between these regions, coupled with an emphasis on the value and quality of the final product, can positively impact consumer perceptions. Marketing campaigns that underscore the global collaboration, showcase the expertise of each region, and align with consumer values contribute to a more favorable perception of the model.

The overall brand image cultivated by companies adopting the "Designed in California, Assembled in China" model plays a pivotal role in shaping consumer attitudes. Beyond the tangible attributes of a product, the brand image encompasses notions of innovation, reliability, and ethical considerations. A positive brand image reinforces the idea that the company is committed to delivering high-quality products, even as it navigates the complexities of globalized manufacturing. Conversely, controversies related to labor practices or environmental concerns can cast a shadow on the brand image, influencing consumer trust and loyalty.

Consumer choices in the context of the "Designed in California, Assembled in China" model are multifaceted, reflecting a delicate interplay of various factors. The perceived quality of the product, brand reputation, and pricing considerations all weigh heavily in the decision-making process. The geographical nuances of the model add an additional layer to these considerations, prompting consumers to reflect on the ethical implications of supporting a globalized manufacturing approach. The resonance of the company's values with those of the consumers, as communicated through its marketing efforts and overall brand image, becomes a pivotal factor in shaping consumer choices.

The evolution of consumer consciousness has brought ethical considerations to the forefront of decision-making processes. Consumers today are increasingly aware of the environmental and social impacts of their purchasing decisions. The "Designed in California, Assembled in China" model prompts consumers to consider the broader ethical implications of their choices. Questions about fair labor practices, the environmental footprint of the manufacturing process, and the overall social responsibility of the company become integral to the decision-making calculus.

Marketing Strategies and Consumer Perceptions:

The marketing strategies deployed by companies utilizing the "Designed in California, Assembled in China" model play a pivotal role in shaping consumer perceptions. Transparency in communicating this manufacturing approach, emphasizing quality, and highlighting the collaborative global effort in bringing products to fruition can positively influence consumer trust. Conversely, a lack of transparency or miscommunication can lead to skepticism and erode consumer confidence.

The brand image associated with the "Designed in California, Assembled in China" model extends beyond the product itself. It encompasses notions of innovation, quality, and the ethical considerations surrounding global manufacturing practices. Companies that successfully align this model with positive brand attributes reinforce the perception of their products as technologically advanced, well-designed, and globally conscious. On the other hand, any controversies related to working conditions or environmental concerns in manufacturing centers can tarnish the brand image and impact consumer loyalty.

Consumers, in the ever-expanding marketplace, navigate a myriad of factors when making purchasing decisions. The perceived quality of the product, brand reputation, pricing, and the alignment of values between consumers and the company all play pivotal roles. The "Designed in California, Assembled in China" model adds another layer to these considerations, as consumers weigh the implications of global manufacturing practices on their choices.

Ethical considerations have emerged as a significant driver in consumer decision-making. The awareness of environmental sustainability, fair labor practices, and the social responsibility of companies has grown exponentially. Consumers increasingly scrutinize the entire supply chain, seeking products that align with their ethical values. The "Designed in California, Assembled in China" model prompts consumers to consider the ethical implications of supporting a globalized manufacturing approach, where labor conditions and environmental practices may vary.

In navigating the consumer perspective of the "Designed in California, Assembled in China" model, it is evident that consumer choices are shaped by a complex interplay of factors. The success of this model lies not only in delivering technologically advanced products but also in aligning with consumer values and ethical considerations. Companies that transparently communicate their manufacturing practices, emphasize quality, and address ethical concerns are better positioned to cultivate consumer trust and loyalty. As the landscape of consumer preferences continues to evolve, the fusion of innovation, brand integrity, and ethical consciousness will define the success of companies embracing the globalized nature of manufacturing.

"Designed in California. Assembled in China. The message is etched elegantly into the many Apple products that I pick up, pocket, and log into daily.

Concept and execution: Different functions managed on opposing sides of the planet but totally integrated.

Apple's success is as much to do with its sourcing and supply chain excellence as its famed design and intuitive operating system. From around the turn of the millennium the bulk of Apple's making has been done offshore. China mainly. But also India and Brazil and other places where components are produced and integrated into the supply chain.

Small(ish) teams of product designers conceive beautiful and easy to use devices. Vast numbers of technicians, and now robots, make the billions of units that part customers from their cash. Steve Jobs, Jony Ive, Tim Cook and their acolytes understood that achieving scale (and world domination) required access to large pools of workers with skills and flexibility, and at price points, not available in California. So, through a magical mix of design, marketing and outsourcing, Apple became the world's most valuable company by market cap." – Mark Hannant (Apple has outsourcing at its core. You can too.)